BALANCING
THE DAILY FAMILY BUDGET
Bill Paying Journal

ACTIVINOTES

Activinotes
DAILY JOURNALS, PLANNERS, NOTEBOOKS AND OTHER BLANK BOOKS

This Book Belongs To

_____

What's Inside

January

DATE	BILL / EXPENSE	AMOUNT	DUE	BALANCE	PAID

Quick Reminders

_____
_____
_____
_____

Priority Bills

_____
_____
_____
_____

DATE	BILL / EXPENSE	AMOUNT	DUE	BALANCE	PAID

Quick Reminders

_____
_____
_____
_____

Priority Bills

_____
_____
_____
_____

DATE	BILL / EXPENSE	AMOUNT	DUE	BALANCE	PAID

Quick Reminders

_____

_____

_____

_____

_____

Priority Bills

_____

_____

_____

_____

_____

DATE	BILL / EXPENSE	AMOUNT	DUE	BALANCE	PAID

Quick Reminders

_____
_____
_____
_____
_____

Priority Bills

_____
_____
_____
_____
_____

DATE	BILL / EXPENSE	AMOUNT	DUE	BALANCE	PAID

Balancing the Daily Family Budget Bill

Quick Reminders

_____

_____

_____

_____

Priority Bills

_____

_____

_____

_____

DATE	BILL / EXPENSE	AMOUNT	DUE	BALANCE	PAID

Balancing the Daily Family Budget Bill

Quick Reminders

_____

_____

_____

_____

Priority Bills

_____

_____

_____

_____

DATE	BILL / EXPENSE	AMOUNT	DUE	BALANCE	PAID

Balancing the Daily Family Budget Bill

DATE	BILL / EXPENSE	AMOUNT	DUE	BALANCE	PAID

February

DATE	BILL / EXPENSE	AMOUNT	DUE	BALANCE	PAID

Quick Reminders

_____
_____
_____
_____

Priority Bills

_____
_____
_____
_____

DATE	BILL / EXPENSE	AMOUNT	DUE	BALANCE	PAID

Quick Reminders

_____
_____
_____
_____

Priority Bills

_____
_____
_____
_____

DATE	BILL / EXPENSE	AMOUNT	DUE	BALANCE	PAID

Balancing the Daily Family Budget Bill

Quick Reminders

_____
_____
_____
_____

Priority Bills

_____
_____
_____
_____

DATE	BILL / EXPENSE	AMOUNT	DUE	BALANCE	PAID

Balancing the Daily Family Budget Bill

DATE	BILL / EXPENSE	AMOUNT	DUE	BALANCE	PAID

Balancing the Daily Family Budget Bill

DATE	BILL / EXPENSE	AMOUNT	DUE	BALANCE	PAID

Quick Reminders

_____

_____

_____

_____

Priority Bills

_____

_____

_____

_____

DATE	BILL / EXPENSE	AMOUNT	DUE	BALANCE	PAID

Quick Reminders		Priority Bills

DATE	BILL / EXPENSE	AMOUNT	DUE	BALANCE	PAID

March

_____
_____
_____
_____

_____
_____
_____
_____

DATE	BILL / EXPENSE	AMOUNT	DUE	BALANCE	PAID

Balancing the Daily Family Budget Bill

DATE	BILL / EXPENSE	AMOUNT	DUE	BALANCE	PAID

Quick Reminders

_____

_____

_____

_____

Priority Bills

_____

_____

_____

_____

DATE	BILL / EXPENSE	AMOUNT	DUE	BALANCE	PAID

Balancing the Daily Family Budget Bill

DATE	BILL / EXPENSE	AMOUNT	DUE	BALANCE	PAID

Balancing the Daily Family Budget Bill

Quick Reminders

_____
_____
_____
_____

Priority Bills

_____
_____
_____
_____

DATE	BILL / EXPENSE	AMOUNT	DUE	BALANCE	PAID

Balancing the Daily Family Budget Bill

Quick Reminders	Priority Bills
_____	_____
_____	_____
_____	_____
_____	_____

DATE	BILL / EXPENSE	AMOUNT	DUE	BALANCE	PAID

Quick Reminders

_____
_____
_____
_____

Priority Bills

_____
_____
_____
_____

DATE	BILL / EXPENSE	AMOUNT	DUE	BALANCE	PAID

Balancing the Daily Family Budget Bill

Quick Reminders

_____
_____
_____
_____

Priority Bills

_____
_____
_____
_____

DATE	BILL / EXPENSE	AMOUNT	DUE	BALANCE	PAID

April

DATE	BILL / EXPENSE	AMOUNT	DUE	BALANCE	PAID

Balancing the Daily Family Budget Bill

_____
_____
_____
_____

_____
_____
_____
_____

DATE	BILL / EXPENSE	AMOUNT	DUE	BALANCE	PAID

Quick Reminders

Priority Bills

DATE	BILL / EXPENSE	AMOUNT	DUE	BALANCE	PAID

Balancing the Daily Family Budget Bill

DATE	BILL / EXPENSE	AMOUNT	DUE	BALANCE	PAID

Balancing the Daily Family Budget Bill

DATE	BILL / EXPENSE	AMOUNT	DUE	BALANCE	PAID

Balancing the Daily Family Budget Bill

DATE	BILL / EXPENSE	AMOUNT	DUE	BALANCE	PAID

Quick Reminders

_____
_____
_____
_____

Priority Bills

_____
_____
_____
_____

DATE	BILL / EXPENSE	AMOUNT	DUE	BALANCE	PAID

Balancing the Daily Family Budget Bill

DATE	BILL / EXPENSE	AMOUNT	DUE	BALANCE	PAID

May

Priority Bills

DATE	BILL / EXPENSE	AMOUNT	DUE	BALANCE	PAID

Quick Reminders	Priority Bills

DATE	BILL / EXPENSE	AMOUNT	DUE	BALANCE	PAID

Quick Reminders

_____

_____

_____

_____

Priority Bills

_____

_____

_____

_____

DATE	BILL / EXPENSE	AMOUNT	DUE	BALANCE	PAID

Balancing the Daily Family Budget Bill

Quick Reminders

_____

_____

_____

_____

Priority Bills

_____

_____

_____

_____

DATE	BILL / EXPENSE	AMOUNT	DUE	BALANCE	PAID

Balancing the Daily Family Budget Bill

Quick Reminders

_____
_____
_____
_____

Priority Bills

_____
_____
_____
_____

DATE	BILL / EXPENSE	AMOUNT	DUE	BALANCE	PAID

Balancing the Daily Family Budget Bill

Quick Reminders

_____
_____
_____
_____

Priority Bills

_____
_____
_____
_____

DATE	BILL / EXPENSE	AMOUNT	DUE	BALANCE	PAID

Quick Reminders

_____
_____
_____
_____

Priority Bills

_____
_____
_____
_____

DATE	BILL / EXPENSE	AMOUNT	DUE	BALANCE	PAID

Balancing the Daily Family Budget Bill

DATE	BILL / EXPENSE	AMOUNT	DUE	BALANCE	PAID

June

Priority Bills

DATE	BILL / EXPENSE	AMOUNT	DUE	BALANCE	PAID

Balancing the Daily Family Budget Bill

Quick Reminders

_____
_____
_____
_____

Priority Bills

_____
_____
_____
_____

DATE	BILL / EXPENSE	AMOUNT	DUE	BALANCE	PAID

Quick Reminders

_____
_____
_____
_____

Priority Bills

_____
_____
_____
_____

DATE	BILL / EXPENSE	AMOUNT	DUE	BALANCE	PAID

Quick Reminders	Priority Bills
_____	_____
_____	_____
_____	_____
_____	_____

DATE	BILL / EXPENSE	AMOUNT	DUE	BALANCE	PAID

Quick Reminders	Priority Bills

DATE	BILL / EXPENSE	AMOUNT	DUE	BALANCE	PAID

Balancing the Daily Family Budget Bill

Quick Reminders	Priority Bills
_____	_____
_____	_____
_____	_____
_____	_____

DATE	BILL / EXPENSE	AMOUNT	DUE	BALANCE	PAID

Quick Reminders

Priority Bills

DATE	BILL / EXPENSE	AMOUNT	DUE	BALANCE	PAID

Quick Reminders

Priority Bills

DATE	BILL / EXPENSE	AMOUNT	DUE	BALANCE	PAID

July

DATE	BILL / EXPENSE	AMOUNT	DUE	BALANCE	PAID

Quick Reminders

Priority Bills

DATE	BILL / EXPENSE	AMOUNT	DUE	BALANCE	PAID

Quick Reminders

_____
_____
_____
_____

Priority Bills

_____
_____
_____
_____

DATE	BILL / EXPENSE	AMOUNT	DUE	BALANCE	PAID

Quick Reminders

Priority Bills

DATE	BILL / EXPENSE	AMOUNT	DUE	BALANCE	PAID

Quick Reminders

_____
_____
_____
_____

Priority Bills

_____
_____
_____
_____

DATE	BILL / EXPENSE	AMOUNT	DUE	BALANCE	PAID

Balancing the Daily Family Budget Bill

Quick Reminders	Priority Bills
_____	_____
_____	_____
_____	_____
_____	_____

DATE	BILL / EXPENSE	AMOUNT	DUE	BALANCE	PAID

Quick Reminders

_____
_____
_____
_____

Priority Bills

_____
_____
_____
_____

DATE	BILL / EXPENSE	AMOUNT	DUE	BALANCE	PAID

Quick Reminders

_____
_____
_____
_____

Priority Bills

_____
_____
_____
_____

DATE	BILL / EXPENSE	AMOUNT	DUE	BALANCE	PAID

August

DATE	BILL / EXPENSE	AMOUNT	DUE	BALANCE	PAID

Balancing the Daily Family Budget Bill

Quick Reminders

_____
_____
_____
_____

Priority Bills

_____
_____
_____
_____

DATE	BILL / EXPENSE	AMOUNT	DUE	BALANCE	PAID

Quick Reminders	Priority Bills
_____	_____
_____	_____
_____	_____
_____	_____

DATE	BILL / EXPENSE	AMOUNT	DUE	BALANCE	PAID

Balancing the Daily Family Budget Bill

Quick Reminders	Priority Bills

DATE	BILL / EXPENSE	AMOUNT	DUE	BALANCE	PAID

Balancing the Daily Family Budget Bill

Quick Reminders

_____
_____
_____
_____

Priority Bills

_____
_____
_____
_____

DATE	BILL / EXPENSE	AMOUNT	DUE	BALANCE	PAID

Balancing the Daily Family Budget Bill

Quick Reminders

_____

_____

_____

_____

Priority Bills

_____

_____

_____

_____

DATE	BILL / EXPENSE	AMOUNT	DUE	BALANCE	PAID

Quick Reminders

Priority Bills

DATE	BILL / EXPENSE	AMOUNT	DUE	BALANCE	PAID

Quick Reminders

Priority Bills

DATE	BILL / EXPENSE	AMOUNT	DUE	BALANCE	PAID

September

Quick Reminders

Priority Bills

DATE	BILL / EXPENSE	AMOUNT	DUE	BALANCE	PAID

Balancing the Daily Family Budget Bill

DATE	BILL / EXPENSE	AMOUNT	DUE	BALANCE	PAID

Quick Reminders

Priority Bills

DATE	BILL / EXPENSE	AMOUNT	DUE	BALANCE	PAID

Balancing the Daily Family Budget Bill

Quick Reminders	Priority Bills
_____	_____
_____	_____
_____	_____
_____	_____

DATE	BILL / EXPENSE	AMOUNT	DUE	BALANCE	PAID

Quick Reminders

_____
_____
_____
_____

Priority Bills

_____
_____
_____
_____

DATE	BILL / EXPENSE	AMOUNT	DUE	BALANCE	PAID

Balancing the Daily Family Budget Bill

Quick Reminders

_____
_____
_____
_____

Priority Bills

_____
_____
_____
_____

DATE	BILL / EXPENSE	AMOUNT	DUE	BALANCE	PAID

Quick Reminders

Priority Bills

DATE	BILL / EXPENSE	AMOUNT	DUE	BALANCE	PAID

Quick Reminders

_____

_____

_____

_____

Priority Bills

_____

_____

_____

_____

DATE	BILL / EXPENSE	AMOUNT	DUE	BALANCE	PAID

October

DATE	BILL / EXPENSE	AMOUNT	DUE	BALANCE	PAID

Balancing the Daily Family Budget Bill

DATE	BILL / EXPENSE	AMOUNT	DUE	BALANCE	PAID

Quick Reminders

Priority Bills

DATE	BILL / EXPENSE	AMOUNT	DUE	BALANCE	PAID

Balancing the Daily Family Budget Bill

DATE	BILL / EXPENSE	AMOUNT	DUE	BALANCE	PAID

Quick Reminders

_____

_____

_____

_____

Priority Bills

_____

_____

_____

_____

DATE	BILL / EXPENSE	AMOUNT	DUE	BALANCE	PAID

Balancing the Daily Family Budget Bill

DATE	BILL / EXPENSE	AMOUNT	DUE	BALANCE	PAID

Quick Reminders

Priority Bills

DATE	BILL / EXPENSE	AMOUNT	DUE	BALANCE	PAID

Quick Reminders

_____
_____
_____
_____
_____

Priority Bills

_____
_____
_____
_____
_____

DATE	BILL / EXPENSE	AMOUNT	DUE	BALANCE	PAID

November

DATE	BILL / EXPENSE	AMOUNT	DUE	BALANCE	PAID

Balancing the Daily Family Budget Bill

Quick Reminders

_____
_____
_____
_____

Priority Bills

_____
_____
_____
_____

DATE	BILL / EXPENSE	AMOUNT	DUE	BALANCE	PAID

Quick Reminders

Priority Bills

DATE	BILL / EXPENSE	AMOUNT	DUE	BALANCE	PAID

Quick Reminders	Priority Bills

DATE	BILL / EXPENSE	AMOUNT	DUE	BALANCE	PAID

Quick Reminders

_____
_____
_____
_____

Priority Bills

_____
_____
_____
_____

DATE	BILL / EXPENSE	AMOUNT	DUE	BALANCE	PAID

Balancing the Daily Family Budget Bill

DATE	BILL / EXPENSE	AMOUNT	DUE	BALANCE	PAID

Quick Reminders

Priority Bills

DATE	BILL / EXPENSE	AMOUNT	DUE	BALANCE	PAID

Quick Reminders

_____

_____

_____

_____

Priority Bills

_____

_____

_____

_____

DATE	BILL / EXPENSE	AMOUNT	DUE	BALANCE	PAID

December

DATE	BILL / EXPENSE	AMOUNT	DUE	BALANCE	PAID

Balancing the Daily Family Budget Bill

Quick Reminders

_____
_____
_____
_____

Priority Bills

_____
_____
_____
_____

DATE	BILL / EXPENSE	AMOUNT	DUE	BALANCE	PAID

Quick Reminders

_____

_____

_____

_____

Priority Bills

_____

_____

_____

_____

DATE	BILL / EXPENSE	AMOUNT	DUE	BALANCE	PAID

Balancing the Daily Family Budget Bill

Quick Reminders	Priority Bills

DATE	BILL / EXPENSE	AMOUNT	DUE	BALANCE	PAID

Balancing the Daily Family Budget Bill

Quick Reminders

_____

_____

_____

_____

Priority Bills

_____

_____

_____

_____

DATE	BILL / EXPENSE	AMOUNT	DUE	BALANCE	PAID

Balancing the Daily Family Budget Bill

Quick Reminders

_____
_____
_____
_____

Priority Bills

_____
_____
_____

DATE	BILL / EXPENSE	AMOUNT	DUE	BALANCE	PAID

Quick Reminders	Priority Bills

DATE	BILL / EXPENSE	AMOUNT	DUE	BALANCE	PAID

Balancing the Daily Family Budget Bill

Quick Reminders

_____

_____

_____

_____

Priority Bills

_____

_____

_____

_____

DATE	BILL / EXPENSE	AMOUNT	DUE	BALANCE	PAID

Quick Reminders

_____
_____
_____
_____

Priority Bills

_____
_____
_____
_____

DATE	BILL / EXPENSE	AMOUNT	DUE	BALANCE	PAID

Balancing the Daily Family Budget Bill

Quick Reminders

Priority Bills

DATE	BILL / EXPENSE	AMOUNT	DUE	BALANCE	PAID

Notes

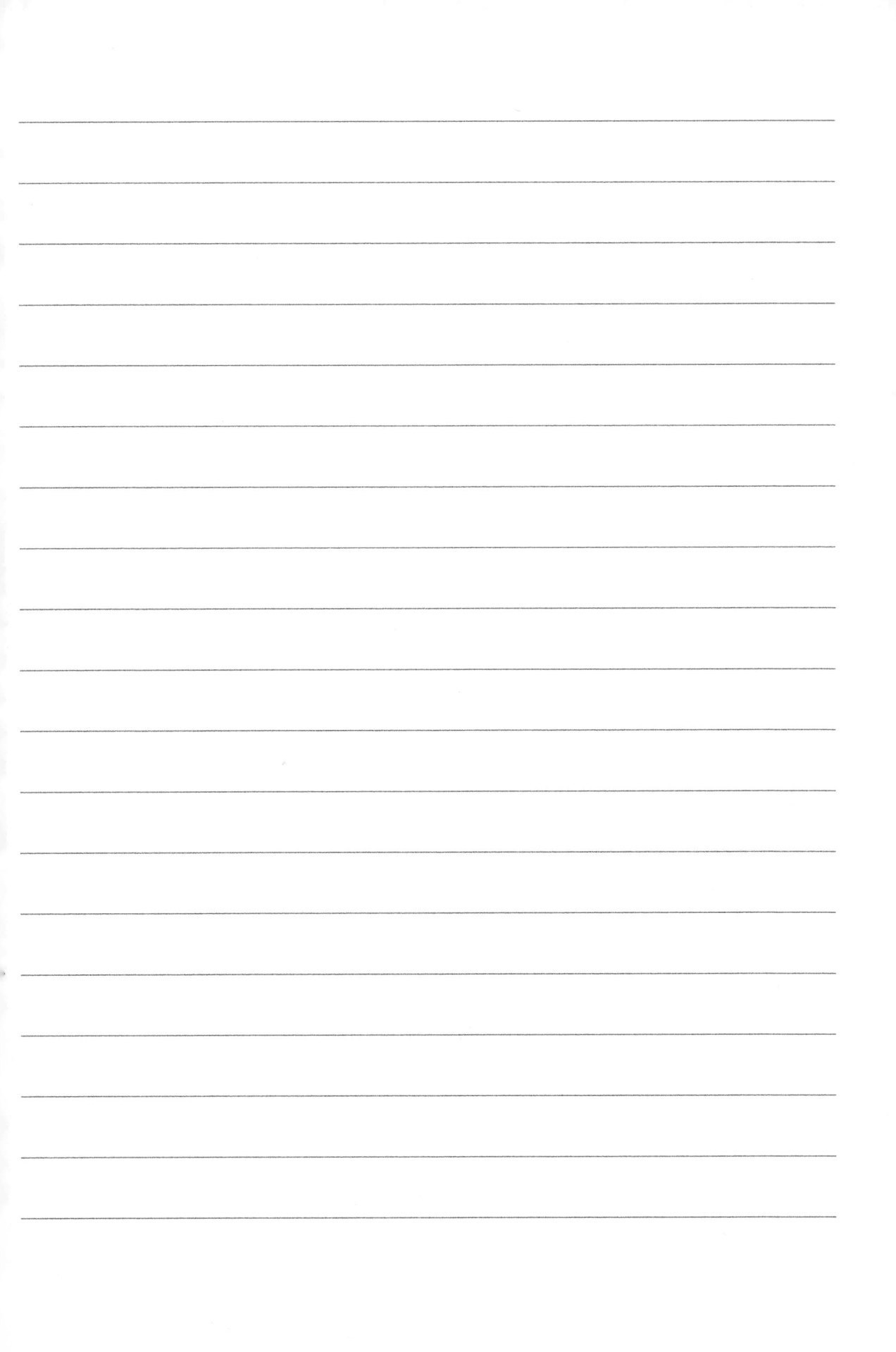

www.ingramcontent.com/pod-product-compliance
Lightning Source LLC
Chambersburg PA
CBHW081333090426
42737CB00017B/3125